T0198837

My Dad will always be with me!

JEREMIAH R. EVANS-WATTS

To order additional copies of this book, contact:
Xlibris
844-714-8691
www.Xlibris.com
Orders@Xlibris.com

ISBN: Softcover   979-8-3694-0265-8
         EBook   979-8-3694-0264-1

Print information available on the last page

Rev. date: 07/06/2023

MY DAD WILL ALWAYS BE WITH ME❣

ME AND MY DAD
DOING HOMEWORK

ME AND MY DAD FISHING

ME AND MY DAD
HAVING LUNCH AT MY SCHOOL.

ME AND MY DAD
AT THE MOVIES.

ME AND MY DAD
WALKING OUR DOG.

ME AND MY DAD
PLAYING VIDEO GAMES.

ME AND MY DAD SKATING.

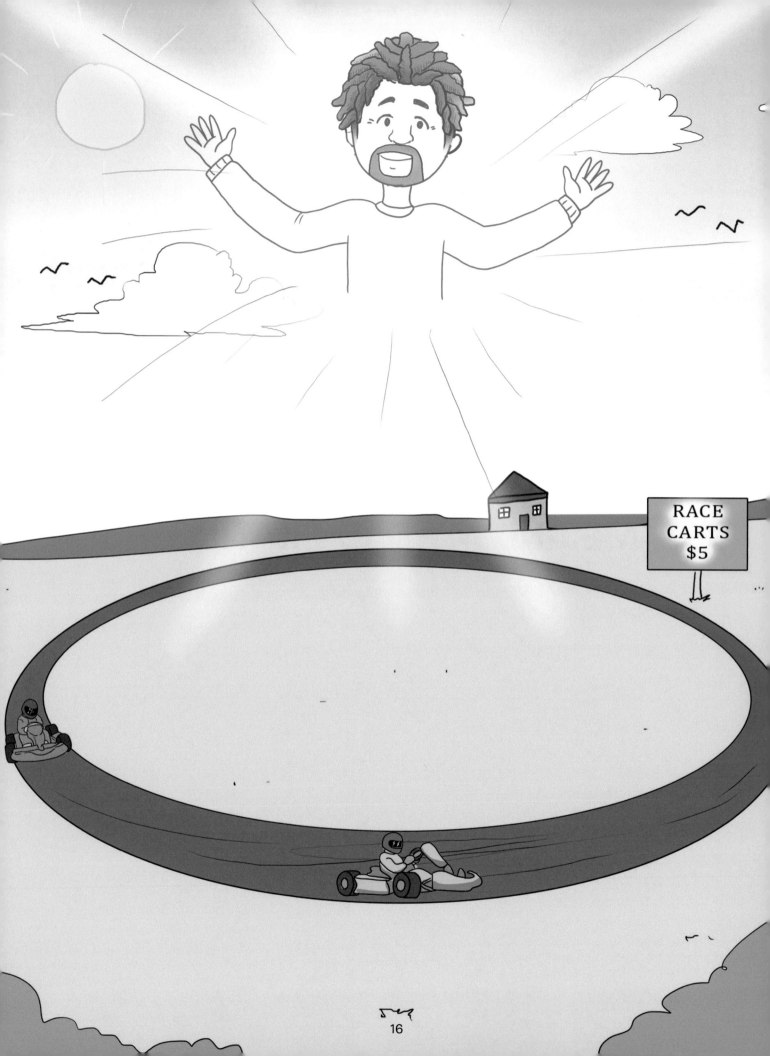

ME AND MY DAD
RACING IN GO-KARTS

ME AND MY DAD
PRAYING IN BEDTIME

DAD THIS IS WHAT YOU AND I ARE DOING UP IN HEAVEN NOW.

Printed in the United States
by Baker & Taylor Publisher Services